ABOUT FIFTEEN PROBLEMS:

Responses to Philosophical Errors

St. Albertus Magnus

Translated by: D.P. Curtin

Dalcassian
Publishing
Company

PHILADELPHIA, PA

ISBN: 978-1-960069-68-9 (Paperback)

Library of Congress Control Number:
Author: Curtin, D.P. (1985-)

Front cover image: *Sermon of Saint Albertus Magnus, Friedrich Walthr, 15th century, The Metropolitan Museum of Art, New York*
Book design by J.J. Ripplestick

Printed by Ingram Content Group, 1 Ingram Blvd, La Vergne, Tennessee

First printing edition 2023.

Master Albert, venerable father in Christ, former bishop of Regensburg, Friar Aegidius of the Order of Preachers, though unworthy of salvation "to glorify the Lord in teaching". The articles proposed in the colleges of the masters of Paris[1], who are considered to be the greatest in philosophy, I have made worthy of transmitting to your authority as one of the illuminating truths of the intellect, so that you may destroy [these errors], having already been struck down in many congregations through the spirit of your words.

---

[1] That is to say, the University of Paris, where Albert was a professor.

Problem I

The understanding of all men is one and the same numerically.

First counterpoint: It is not possible to know the intellect of man according to its nature, both in substance and definition, unless both the nature of the intelligence and the nature and substance of the soul, as well as its definition are known. For we are speaking here of the knowledge which is through philosophy, and not that which is according to faith and theology. Although this is known to all, it is not understood by many. It is thought that those who contribute to theology wish to escape difficulties. Therefore, assuming from the inner aspects of philosophy, [that is] the nature of the intellect, we will speak of the intellect.

In the philosophy of the Peripatetics[2], we find nothing but two new positions, both very different from one another, as well as one ancient one, in which the Peripatetics do not differ, but uniformly agree. The one in which all agree is the position of Anaxagoras[3], who spoke of the potential intellect, says that the potential intellect is separate and unmixed, the simplest, having nothing in common with anyone. For this reason they have thought that something is itself one and the same in all things, and that nothing is properly determined to be one, by which it is not determined to be separate. For if something is determined to one thing, as they say, it necessarily differs from something else. Now this is evident by what can be observed. It is not of the nature of understanding which is common to all. Neither then can it be determined, or rather, it is determined by some other means. Yet, if it is not determined, its purpose is deferred, namely, that it is one and the same in all. If something else is determined which is not of the nature of the intellect, this will be seen to be contrary to the hypothesis, because when nothing is determined by something

---

[2] The school of philosophy founded by Aristotle in 335 BC.

[3] The pre-Socratic philosopher who posited the existence of the cosmic mind, and the homogeneity of the natural world.

which is homogenous, it follows that the intellect is mixed with something, and does not correspond to its position.

Even still, if the intellect is determined by its nature, it will be separated from all others who do not partake of that same nature. Since all knowledge is based on the similarity [between objects], it follows that it can have no complete sense of knowledge of things it is separated from by dissimilarity. Yet, this is entirely false, since the intellect is contingent, by which all things are made intelligible.

This is, therefore, the ancient position held by the Peripatetics, by which Alfarabius[4] elucidated it. It thereafter follows that the intellect of all species is intelligible, and there is not a potential substance with which it is derived. Yet, we are speaking to philosophers, who ought to be prepared to discuss such things, we cannot hold to these forever.

Subsequently, these wise Greeks, namely Porphyrius, Eustratius[5], and Michael of Ephesus[6], and many others besides Alexander who agree with Epicurius, who said that man's understanding is secured by the intellect and does not exist by nature of intelligence alone. For what those wise Greeks possessed, the same Arab philosophers, Avicenna, Averroes, Abubacher and others, said that which is secured is obtained, for that which is secured is different and of a different nature of its securer. As they say, since the soul of the intellectual man is in the image of the whole of the world, and is alone in perceiving all the world, the form which was assigned the natural body by the uniformity of nature is necessary for it to be in the image of that great intelligence which is the tenth world. That world is a sphere of the active and the passive, whose instruments of intelligence are hot and cold, moist and dry, thin and dense, and all those things which are found in the elements, and not within themselves, insofar as

---

[4] That is to say al-Farabi, the Islamic scholar known as the father of Islamic Neoplatonism.

[5] Presumably, this is Eustratius of Nicaea, the famed aristotelian scholar at the University of Constantinople

[6] A later Byzantine scholar who wrote commentaries on Aristotle

these are shaped by the movements of the celestial power. Yet, the image of such intelligence cannot be relegated to the pure and simple, as was the nature of the first and primitive intelligence. For if it were as such, it would not be a natural form first and foremost, as the nature of primitive intelligence is not natural. Therefore, Averroes says, that all the diversity within the body is from the diversity that is in its form, just as the diversity of the organs originates in the range of the powers and forces within the soul. If the soul was said to be without its own powers, then there would be a diversity of powers from the variety of the organs of the body. It would then follow that it could itself utilize any organ for itself, since according to itself it was not determined to be differentiated. Just the same would the tectonics of wearing pipes and other incongruities, which Articles had debated against Pythagoras.

From this position it follows that, just as the intelligence of the lower world is related to the intelligences of the higher worlds, so the intellectual soul, which is in man, is related to the intelligences of the higher worlds. It is, therefore, just as the intelligence of the lower world is formally possessed and acquired by the higher intelligences, which informs it for intellectual operations. So is it in the soul, where the lights of the mind, acquired and possessed by the illumination of those knowable things, are the intellect of the last order, and relates to the power of the elements. The soul, therefore, relates to the distinctions and operations of the organs.

Yet, if someone should say that it is not intelligence that works in the living sphere, but only nature- whoever says this does not know philosophy. For the whole work of nature is proved to be the work of intelligence, by the fact that it forms and works, with the reason of its own end different things, both in plants and in animals, and in all things that are perfect in nature. Nature alone cannot do this, because nature is only for a single thing. For this reason also the soul, which does not reach the perfection of the image of the intellect, except in that part in which intelligence is compared to the virtues of the elements, such as the sensible and the vegetative, and is reduced from the great variety to one and does not follow the great variety which is imagined. And therefore every swallow makes a nest in one way, and every spider makes a web in the same way. Yet, not every man makes his house, or his clothes, or any other of his works, in the same way as others.

From these, and of sheer necessity, it follows that man's understanding is possessed and acquired by a higher nature. It is from such a nature, which is substantially identical to the soul, which is naturally imparted. The more the soul turns away from the inferior power with which it relates to the organs, the more it acquires and possesses its own understanding. What is more, the more it is turned to the organs, the more it is overshadowed and falls from the intellect, and becomes beastly and arboreal, and loses the intellect and declines from the true nature of man. And this is what Aristotle said, that "according to prudence, this understanding does not seem to be equally present in animals, but not in men." And in this most noble attainment, all the Peripatetics said that it was the root of immortality, and that through it men were transposed and transformed into gods, just as in Plato's philosophy they called such heroes demigods.

And from these things it is easily understood, that since the image of the intellect is, from that part in which it is compared to the elementary qualities, neither of one nature, nor of one power, nor of one purity, then the soul of anyone is not the soul of another, therefore possessing in one is not the same as possessing in to another. Now if it is necessary to grant this, since the possessed and the acquired differ according to being according to possession and acquisition, it necessarily follows that the understanding of the possessed and the acquired according to being differ singularly in each. A very appropriate example of this is what Aristotle says in *De Anima, II*: "For although it is transparent in fire, air, water, certain stones, and glass from its conformity with a perpetually superior body, it still differs in its singular being in each of them."

Therefore, according to this position, it does not follow that there is one intellect in number according to the being of every man, but rather that according to being it differs singularly in each of them. Yet, whether in all worlds there are intelligences differing according to their substance, or whether there is in all the light of the first cause operating in the manner of intelligence, differing in them according to the essence which it has in them, as the Avenalpetrans[7] seems to feel, for the present there is no time to discuss this, because each of them said it is always held of necessity that there is not one possible intellect in all men, and this we intend in claim here.

Yet, Avicebron[8], in the book which he called *The Fountain of Life*, proceeded in a different way. For although he professed to be a Peripatetic, he followed the dogmas of the Stoics, and especially that of Plato, desiring to produce all things from one, through his teleological understanding. For this reason, he was distinguished in a threefold matter, namely, that which is first determined by substantial form, and that which is determined by the first corporeal form, and that which is determined by first contrariety. Now, he says that the first form is the intellect or intellectuality, from which he says that intellectual substances and souls are multiplied. Yet, by quantity he says the determinate matter of the heavenly bodies. By contrast he says that the matter of the generable and corruptible physical bodies is determined. And according to this position it is plain that every intellectual nature accepted in this or that is singular, and that there is not one intellect in number, and in some several.

It is evident from all the positions that this is false, even according to philosophy, that a singular number of understanding ontologically is accepted in all. In many, it is multiplied within them, and the being which it has in one, it does not have in another.

---

[7] This appears to be correctly broken as Aven Alpetrans, or the disciples of the Arab astronomer Nur ad-Din al-Bitruji, also known as Alpetragius in the Latin world. This citation is a point of curiosity, as his works must have circulated the Mediterranean relatively quickly.

[8] That is to say, Solomon ibn Gabirol Avicebron the Jewish Neo-platonic philosopher from Muslim Spain.

Yet, what Anaxagoras says, that it has nothing in common with anyone, was said of the nature and essence of the intellect, and not of its being. For it is certain that according to its being the intellect is connected with continuity and to time. Therefore, those things which are connected with continuity and time are mixed in many and many ways. And the example of all these is the transparent in nature, in the sky, fire and air and water, stones and glass.

Therefore, what they say is not only false according to the theologians, but also according to philosophy. The cause of this is said to be the ignorance of the philosophers, because many of the Parisians[9] did not follow philosophy, but sophistry.

This, then, is the answer to the first question.

Problem II
That these things are false or improper, to say "man understands them."

The second is that they say this is false or improper: "man understands." He did not say this unless he was ignorant of philosophy and of himself, because it is determined in philosophy that man alone has an intellect, and that understanding is a proper and connatural activity of mankind, which, if not hindered, is man's highest joy. By which, it is clear that there is nothing in the world so proper as this: "man understands." For since it is true to speak of that thing that belongs to everything, and to itself. As Boethius says, that truth flows from substance and substantial things, it is not proper for man to feel and to be vegetarian, but only to understand it.

---

[9] Here Albert is directly targeting the faculty members of the University of Paris, and not the denizens of Paris in particular.

Still, since there is no proposition truer than that in which a connatural and proper act is attributed to him whose proper and connatural act is evident. So, that among all propositions there is none truer than this: "man understands". As when it is said: light shines, and sight is white. It breaks apart. It is hot, and all the like. Unless perhaps he wants to say that man's understanding is nothing, which is very absurd. For it follows from the fact that man is man, that there is nothing of man, which no one has ever thought, because this is not intelligible. For everything that is distinguished from other species of its kind must have some ultimate and reversible difference, which it essentially participates in, to be distinguished from others, as was inevitably proved in *Primae Philosophiae, VII*. Yet, the intellectual life is the ultimate difference of man, as all the Stoics and Peripatetics confess.

If by chance they say that the intellect is in man as nature and power, but has no act and operation in him, this is absolutely absurd, because it follows that the proper nature is destitute of operation, which also is absurd.

Yet. if by chance they say that it is the proper act of a man to reason and not to understand, this is not the saying of a very unskilled man, but a simpleton. Since if one looks more closely at these things, reasoning never takes place unless it is informed by the understanding of the component and division of a thing. Therefore the intellect is according to nature and reason. Therefore it is more characteristic of man to understand than to reason.

Yet, if he wants to say that understanding belongs to the higher nature as it belongs to the angelic nature and therefore cannot be proper to the lower, the first thing is contrary to this, that the philosopher runs outside the goals of philosophy, because he is not philosophical. The distinctions of the angels were accepted by the revelation of the spirit and not by philosophy. But if he says that according to philosophy there are orders of intelligences, and it belongs to them and not to man to understand, and this again is absurd, because nothing prevents what is said by analogy from being proper in several different ways.

But if this is meant, as some Arab philosophers have said, that the intellect of a person acts outside the soul, which is like the sun and as "art supported by matter", then this is a very weak statement, because it does not follow from this given that a man cannot understand properly and truly. Yet, since the intelligence which is like the sun alone shining and forming all things to be, and to shine and like the art of matter influences the forms of art from itself, the influence of the light of that intelligence through being is in the soul and thus informs the soul to the understanding and the operation of its understanding, just as the sun all informs the light to the form and operation of illumination. As they are properly and truly called luminaries and having the act of shining, so they are properly named, intellectuals, have the operation of the intellect, because that which is the act of the superior does not prevent, according to its shared being, the substantial difference of the inferior nature, as is evident in all that generate through form and substance . Still, although we say so by supporting the position, it has not been proved that what they say is true.

Therefore, what they said in the second fiction is absolutely absurd.

Question III

What the will of man wills and chooses is out of necessity.

What they say thirdly, that the will of man wills and chooses out of necessity, could never be said unless a man was completely illiterate, because every reason and every school of ethics, both Stoics and Peripatetics, claims that we are masters of our actions and therefore praiseworthy or blameworthy. Now the Philosophers, who speak of the nature of the soul, distinguish the soul from nature in this respect, because nature is by itself one, but the soul is by itself the operation of many things, and is also selective of opposites and contradictions. None of which is true, if a man wills what he wills out of necessity and chooses out of necessity what he chooses.

Furthermore, if what they say is true, the will is no longer the will, which is clear from Hermes Trismegistus and Aristotle and from all those who distinguished causes into ten orders, in which distinction the will is always distinguished from necessity.

Still, according to this, fortune is not about those things which are done by purpose, because fortune does not admit of necessity, and thus a great part of the *Metaphysics* is false.

The fact that they associate election with the will, which is never of the will, was not at all philosophical. And further, to put it briefly, it is so absurd that it is not worthy of an answer.

If they say this because of fate and the constellations, which the poet says necessarily drag the will. As the poet says: "Your fates drag you, so that you cannot leave what you have begun". This is the saying of the ignorant and the solace of the malicious. It is proved at the beginning of the book, which in Arabic is called *Alarba*, but in Latin is called *Quadripartitum*[10], that fate, which is from a constellation, does not impose necessity for three reasons. One of these is that it does not come immediately, but through a medium, whose inequality can be hindered. The second, works by accident, but not by itself, but in those who are born. For it works through the first qualities, which do not of themselves receive the virtues of the stars. The third is that it works in that in which it works, in the variety and power of the matter of the children, which matter uniformly and, as they are in the heavens, cannot receive the virtues of the heavens. In every way, then, what they say is ridiculous.

Question IV

All that is done in the lower things is subject to the necessity of the heavenly bodies.

What they bring forth in the fourth place, that all that is done in the lower things is subject to the necessity of the heavenly bodies, has almost the same form of disproof. It is surprising, however, that the professors of philosophy say against those things which have been proven by philosophy. For if the sixth book of the first philosophy is read[11], it is easy to see how things that are done in the lower are subject to the government of the higher. For there it is shown how that which is frequently and not always and everywhere in natural causes falls from that which is always, and does not attain the necessity of that which is always. It is also proved how that which is rare in chance and fortune falls from that which is frequent, and does not attain its order. In order that their ignorance may be entirely manifest, it is proved in *De Generatione et Corruptione, II* that although the rising of the sun and the planets in the circle of declination is the cause of lower generation, and the retreat of the same in the same circle is the cause of corruption. They are equal in the period of generation and corruption. The lower periods are equal and they do not achieve order because of the inequality and disorder of matter. But who doubts that the purpose of man is more unequal and disordered than that of nature? Therefore purpose is much less subject to necessity than to nature.

Since, as Aristotle says, it is not enough to show a falsity, unless the cause of the falsity is also shown. We therefore summarize by saying that the human soul, according to Philosophers, is the image of the world. Because of this, in that part in which the image of the intelligence and the first cause is, it is impossible to subject it to the motions of the heavenly bodies. In that part which is in the organs, although it is moved by the scintillations of the stars, yet it does not attain the necessity and order of the superiors, and thus neither is it subject to

---

[10] Better known as Ptolemy's Tetrabiblos, this is simply the Latin rendering of the same title.

[11] Nicomachean Ethics by Aristotle

necessity or is subject to the superiors in that part. And this is proved by Haly[12] in his Commentary on the Centiloquium of Ptolema, who says that a king whose all signifiers were evil and impure, and yet, born under such a constellation, he lived most cleanly, resplendent in dress and glory, conversing with the best. When Haly was asked the reason for this, he replied that he was indeed drawn to impurity by desire, but seeing that such was the dishonorable conversation, that the master of his actions, fleeing from such things, chose the conversation of honesty.

Another example is in the Physiognomy of Poles from Hippocrates. For in all the signs of the body, which Ptolemy calls the second stars, Hippocrates appeared to be a harlot and an ugly person, and yet he was of the best of studies and of the most honorable conduct. So much so that he was called the best of all men, which could not be done except by the choice of honesty. Therefore, they do not impose a necessity on the lower ones on the higher ones, and not one of the mathematicians ever said this. For if this were so, chance would perish, free will would perish, counsel would perish, and contingency would perish according to the whole scope of its community, which is very absurd.

Problem V

That the world is eternal.

Now that the world is eternal, as they introduce in the fifth question, is a very ancient question, although it cannot be held from the proof of Aristotle, but that the first movement was made by no generative power and can cease by no physical corruptor. And this is best disproved by Moses of Egypt[13] in the Book called *The Leader of the Neutrals*. For although they are ingenerable and incorruptible, which is from their whole matter, yet it is undeniable that every multitude ordered to one in all motions is caused by the first one, who is the

---

[12] That is Haly ibn Rodoan

[13] Better known to history as the Jewish doctor Moses Maimonides

cause of that order. Now all the multitude of the orbs and stars in all their motions look to one and the same thing, in respect of which all movable things are continually changing in their forms, although according to themselves fully, and according to all the parts do not move according to their place. Now this is both the center and the pole. For the center and the poles are referred to one and the same axis, which most astronomers call. Therefore, there is a necessary cause of this order, whatever it may be.

Now it has been proved that there is no local motion except from some active catalyst, which by giving form also gives motion. Therefore, that which ascribes motion to the heavenly things must be that which generates them according to the same matter and form. The heavens, therefore, with all that is in it, was born according to substance and nature, and thus the position which they say is disproved.

Now if someone says that this is true of things that are naturally moved and not of things that are moved by the soul, this is hocum, because the movement of the superiors is not only from the soul, according to those who claim to have superior souls. For if it were from the soul alone and not from nature, it would also cause weariness of the bodies, according to those who are professors of this position. Since, then, the movement of the corporeal nature is the same as that resulting from their nature and form, it follows by necessity what has already been concluded before.

For this reason, even the philosophers themselves, such as Avicenna and Algazelle[14], say that it is not forbidden that the world was made by creation, although motion and movement were not first made through physical generation and although there is no cessation through physical decay. There are many more about this question in *Aliis Scriptus (Other Writings)* of mine, and therefore these will suffice.

However, this also applies to what was proved in *Arithmeticae, II*[15] in the place called invincible, namely that all multiplicity is reduced to unity, which is the substantial cause of that multiplicity. Let us inquire further then, to what is reduced before it all the multiplicity of the heavens and stars and motions. And it is clear to every one that it cannot be reduced except to the unity of the prime mover, which all the inferiors in their motions in some measure desire.

If, however, one examines carefully what is the cause of that deformed desire, one cannot say that it is other than an imperfect likeness to the first cause. Since something does not desire another except through the likeness which it bears to another. Nor can we say that anything can be moved to anything else except because of the imperfection which it has in that which it desires. Therefore, the likeness of the first, which is in all things and is manifold, could not be caused in them except by the fact that all things are from him. For all things of which there is an essential likeness to one, flow from someone, in which that in which they are like is actual and perfect. So are species from their genus, and so are individuals from their species, so all multiplicity draws itself into unity. Let us ask them, then, if anyone could understand this, that first of all this likeness flows into all things already existing in nature and being. It is clear that this is not intelligible. It must therefore be that he caused this likeness in all things, causing all things according to their essence and into a natural and substantial being. All things, therefore, are perfected by one, according to their substantial and natural being. Therefore, all things were made according to being. Therefore, they are not eternal in this way, because they did not have the principle of being according to substance and nature.

---

[14] A misspelling of Al-Ghazal, the Arab diplomat famed in his own lifetime

[15] Presumably Albert is alluding to the work by Diophantus

Problem VI

That there was never the first man.

The sixth, which they propose, is not philosophical. For the philosopher is to say what he says with reason. Yet, this cannot be proved, that is, that there never was a first man, and that he was at one time the first man. Since neither of these propositions can be proved by reason, it is more probable that there once was one first man than that there was not. However, man, like any of the perfect animals, is not of those things which can be born by putrefaction, as Averroes says on *Metaphysics, XI.* Therefore, no human being naturally entered into human existence except through his generation. Yet, in every generation the begetting is determined. Every man, therefore, has a determinate catalyst. However, the begetting of all that is determinate was at one time in the appointed time. Every man, therefore, was at some time in the great limit of time. Yet, from the infinite there is nothing to accept that which is limited. Since all things are infinite, which do not happen to pass through to what is signified, therefore in those things which are signified and determined, it is not necessary to posit infinity, but it is necessary to posit something first.

If it may be said that from the constellation different generations are made in different principles of habitation, this again is contrary to the philosophy which says that the most perfect animals cannot be born from the constellations alone. For this reason Plato in the first book of the *Timaeus* and Ovid, speaking of the floods of the elements, which occur because of the exorbitant of the stars, say that Pyrrha[16] and Deucalion[17] were reserved, from whom the future seed of the human generation would be reserved. Now, since man is the image of the first cause, it is more probable that the first man was determined to be from the first cause, than that he proceeded into being in some other way.

---

[16] The mythological Queen of Thessaly, daughter of Pandora, the Greeks as a nation were said to be her descendants

[17] Deucalion is the ancient Greek equivalent of the myth of Noah and the antediluvian patriarchs.

And let us use the probability of Aristotle himself, which Tullius[18] states in *On the Nature of the gods- Book I*, where he quotes the words of Aristotle, saying that if a palace is suddenly found standing in the desert, in which nothing but swallows are to be found, although the artist who made the palace is not known, yet from He himself is immediately convinced by the arrangement of the palace, that the swallows did not make that palace, but that some intellectual nature made it by the method of his own art. Even so, since the world is the work of art and reason, and cannot consist of its own generation, it is only probable that the first generated substances were brought into existence by the reasonings of God or the gods. And this is certainly the philosophy of Aristotle, which he himself calls vulgar in *The Heavens and the Earth-Book I*. It is more reasonable, then, that the first man came into being through creation, than that there never was a first man.

Problem VII

The soul, which is the form of man, according to what man is, is corrupted by a corrupt body.

And what they say seventhly, the soul, which is the form of man, according to which man is corrupted by a corrupt body, proceeds from ignorance of all kinds of philosophy, because according to the philosophers[19], nothing that is truly form is corrupted, because it is not in matter. For that which is in matter is either an image of form or a resonance.

Furthermore, if that alone is truly form, which is not the act of any matter, it follows that the intellect alone is truly form, inasmuch as it is the act of no person. Now the understanding is the form of man, as man is, which is

---

[18] That is to say, the Roman orator, Cicero

[19] Here he appears to be specific to Platonic philosophy

separated as incorruptible from corruptible. Therefore the form of man, as man is, is not corruptible.

However, if they want to say that there is a soul, which is the entelechy[20] or act of the body, what they say is utter ignorance. For the soul is the entelechy of the body through its substantial act, which is life, as is clear from another definition of the soul, which is a "demonstration differing in position." That is to say: "the soul is the principle and cause of life, according to which to live is to be in the living." And yet not all the parts of the body partake of life in one way, but some to be nourished and vegetated, and some to feel, and some more, some less, yet all partake in life.

Let us inquire, therefore, whether they partake in the life of the understanding or not. And if it be said that it is not, it necessarily follows that the soul, which is the form of man, has a body for sense and vegetation and not for understanding. Therefore, the body of man will not be proper to the rational soul, and thus it follows that "I put on tectonic pipes."

For this reason, it is necessary to say that all the members live in the rational soul, just as all the tools of the weaver are formed for the work of the weaver, and that sense in man is not a form, but a power of the rational soul, and the same must be said of the vegetative. Hence, it is that the flesh of man differs in appearance from the flesh of other animals.

From this it follows that either the whole is corrupted according to the substantial act, or, if it is saved according to the substance, that it is also saved according to the whole of that which is the form of man, as man is. However, he is saved according to his substance, as Aristotle says in *Metaphysics, XI* and in many other places, and we have proved this in the book *On the Immortality of the Soul*. It is necessary, therefore, that it should be saved according to all

---

[20] A more formalized way of discussing human potential, particularly as it relates to the human soul

things which are in it as its powers. Yet, it is vegetative in the sensible, and sensible in the rational "as a trigon in a tetragon." Therefore the vegetable and the sensible are saved by some means. But they cannot be saved in any other way, except as they are in the rational, as in the power of it. Therefore, the soul of man is saved, as it is vegetative and sensitive in itself, not as an act, but as a rational power of the soul.

This statement, then, was not wisely said, because the whole soul of man, even in the bones, is not the form of man, except as it is rational, infusing the life of reason into all the members. For this reason, Aristotle says that the hand is the organ of the understanding. And just as there is nothing but the form of the intellect in the ax and the ax and the tools and in gold, wood and stone, so the form of the rational soul is just as there is a rational form in all the members of the human body. This, indeed, is separated according to substance and a certain operation, but in certain operations it is separated according to power and not according to operation, just as art is separated from the operation of the ax and the swinging of the ax, although it is saved according to its power. Therefore, this statement was not according to philosophy.

Now whether the soul is corruptible or not is not relevant to the proposed intention, because we are not asking about nature, but arguing against a certain position. This is the reason why theologians say that even human bodies receive the power of incorruption from the immortal soul. For there is no form which does not complete and terminate all the matter due to it in order to be proper to the form and act and operation. Nor is there any instance of this proposition. Therefore, everything that is actually a part of man is determined to be the rational soul and the act and operation of the rational soul. Whence the vegetated flesh is acting as such by the vegetative nature of man to the act of the living rational being, and the sense feels to the act of the living rational. Otherwise it would not be for the intelligent to understand, which is inappropriate, because it has been proved *In Naturalibus*[21] that, just as living is for the living to be and to feel for the sentient, so to understand is to be for the intelligent. Now the rational soul is separated as the incorruptible from the corruptible. Then it is separated either according to its whole substance or according to a part of its substance. Nor can it be said that it is separated according to the part of its substance, because nothing simple, that is, not of quantity, is separated according to the part of its substance. By the same token, nor can it be understood that a part of a substance is separated and not the whole in such things as are not extended by the bulk of quantity. Therefore, the whole substance of the soul, which is the form of the human body, is separated, although in the separated soul some of the powers are not separated according to their being, which they have in the body, as is clear from what has been said.

If these ancients would like to be disciples of the new error, which was derived from Plato, and would say that the vegetable, the sensible, and the rational are the three substances which are in man, this is easily eliminated by the *First Philosophy*. For according to this the definition of man, by which he is called living, sensible, and rational, would be many and not one. For in saying this, the living is not in the sensible by being sensible, and the sensible is not in the rational by being rational, but there will be three distinct substances, none of which is in another by being. If it is said by someone, he must be expelled from the schools of philosophy because of his ignorance, because such a person is certain to be ignorant of the very principles of philosophy.

But if it is said that the Philosopher himself says in *Metaphysics, XI* that the whole soul of man is not separated, it is certain that the Philosopher does not say this because the whole substance is not separated, but because the whole is not separated according to the being of the powers.

---

[21] It's not clear what work he is alluding to, perhaps *Physics* by Aristotle

Problem VIII

That the separated soul after death does not suffer from bodily fire.

Eighthly, they say that the separated soul does not suffer from bodily fire after death. Yet, this is in no way philosophical, since, according to Socrates at the end of the book called the *Phaedo,* the infernals are distinguished as places of punishment, and infernal rivers, and places of goods adorned with glittering jewels. Isaac[22] also imitated this manner in the *Book of Definitions,* and many poets also sang such passages in a philosophical song, which is called a story.

Let them say, then, whether the rational soul suffers anything in the body or not. If indeed he does not suffer, then he is completely impervious to pain, since pain is the opposite of dissolving the senses. Yet, if he suffers, it is evident that he suffers bodily pain. Therefore, since it is outside the body of the same nature as it is in the body, it is clear that even outside the body it can suffer from bodily afflictions.

If by chance they say that the soul has the opposite in the body, but not stripped of the body, this is not true according to all philosophy, because it is determined in philosophy that the end of the prosperity of the separated soul, which is the ultimate happiness, and that it is united to the first mover. Now it is clear that, according to all the Stoics, it is a sin to separate from the first mover, and this is the opposite of union. Therefore, the naked soul has something opposite. Therefore, just as it hurts on the contrary in the body, so it hurts on the contrary outside the body.

Still, it cannot be proved that the soul does not grieve over bodily suffering, because this is contrary to the test of the senses. The apprehension of the afflicted as the afflicted causes internal pain of the soul. Therefore, even the apprehension of the afflicted outside the body causes internal pain of the soul.

---

[22] That is Isaac Israeli, the physician for the Fatimid dynasty, composer of various medical and philosophical works.

What is the reason, then, that it is said that, undressed, he does not grieve for bodily affliction? And this is what Gregory[23] says, that this is to burn in the fire, that to see the fire, this is to take hold of the afflicted.

If he wants to say that the body cannot react to animal pain, this is completely absurd, because in the natural heat, which is fire, we see actions to the sense of the soul, both delighting and saddening, because although such heat is fiery, it is nevertheless informed by the soul and the movement of the soul drives the operations and passions. What, then, prevents bodily fire from receiving power from the first mover, inasmuch as it is the instrument of it, which acts upon the animal soul and not by bodily action or passion? Nor is there anything of the kind against the philosophy of the Stoics or even of the Peripatetics, but such proceed either from ignorance or at least from hatred of faith rather than from proven truth.

Problem IX

That free will is a passive power, not active, and which is of necessity moved by desire.

What the ninth says, that free will is a passive and not an active power, and therefore necessarily moved by the appetitive, is completely absurd and contrary to the principles of the ethical philosophers. For those powers which are called passive in the soul are said to be receptive, as is clear from the book *De Anima, III.* Acceptance is never accomplished without action, and therefore such powers cannot be simply passive. For such powers contribute to themselves, and from themselves to the forms that are in them, just as the visible form contributes to itself and from its own transparency, which is in itself only according to the being of light and the transparent. And in this way the understanding and every part of reception contributes to the form and acts

---

[23] Likely, he is alluding to St. Gregory of Nyssa, although the reference appears to be obscure.

in it the truth and simplicity, which in itself is the intelligible form. When the intellect communicates from the appetitive to the appetite, it is evident that also that which is the appetite is communicated to the appetitive, which is itself in the appetite. Such an operation is said by philosophers to be a perfect and not an imperfect act, because motion would not be an imperfect act of some kind unless it were also a perfect act of some kind. For it is a perfect act of mover and agent, but an imperfect act of mover and sufferer. Since, therefore, the principles constituting the form, as intellectual and appetitive, are the intellect and the appetite itself, such powers, from which such principles of forms flow, are rather active than passive, and what is more, they are simply active and in a sense passive. This is the reason why we are masters of our actions. Therefore, the principle of such is in us and from us. Therefore, it is not necessarily motivated by desire.

And still such a pseudo-philosopher destroys continence and the whole of *Nicomachean Ethics, VII*, because the continence is moved by a base passion, but is not led away, abstaining from the pursuit of the passions through free will. And the error befalls him, just as it did Theophrastus[24], because the passions of the soul are measured by physical passions, when they have nothing in common with them, as is the case with all those who are well versed in ethical philosophies.

Problem X

God does not know the particulars.

But what is said in the tenth, that God does not know particulars, proceeds from all kinds of ignorance. For it is supposed that the knowledge of God is unequivocal to the knowledge of man, which is disproved in *First Philosophy*. For all my knowledge is caused by things, as you know, because all our knowledge is caused by reasons of things and passions. For this reason all science is better than the science of resolution, which the Greeks call analytic, while either the compound is resolved into the simple, or the caused into the cause, or generally the latter is resolved into the former. For the knowledge of composition in man is caused by resolution, because he does not know how to compose, except he who knows the components and the proportions of the components to each other and to the compounds. Hence it is necessary that the knowledge of resolution be first, and that of composition second. But every resolution is accomplished by abstraction. Therefore, human knowledge is through abstraction. But abstraction is made from things and cannot be done otherwise. Therefore, man's knowledge is caused by things. Now the knowledge of God is not made of things but is the cause of things. For it is clear that every form is the light of intelligence, because since every form is given by the intellect, which is the intellect according to its substance and essence, and not by the intellect, which is called acquired or acquired or possessed by the philosophers, it must be that every form is caused by the universally acting intellect. the forms of all intelligible things. How this is to be done is not possible except in this way, that the light of the active intellect itself is the form of that which is constituted by the inner intellect, which is universally active. But every understanding which establishes a thing into being and form, is first to the particular, and secondly to the universal, in which nature acts as a result of the hidden. Therefore, the understanding of God and the divine knowledge are first of the particular, and if they are of the universal, this will be not first, but as a consequence. For this is what the philosopher means when he says that such an understanding is like the sun and "like art sustained to matter." For the sun is constitutive of the visible in particular, and art constitutive of artificial things in particular, and not in the universal except as a consequence.

Moreover, every form of a thing is made intelligible by this understanding, or possession of it, because it is the light of the agent-intellect, which is the proper act of the possible intellect, just as every color is visible, because it is the act of the light of the sun, which is the proper act of the visual power. It is necessary,

---

[24] The successor to Aristotle at the Lyceum

therefore, that every form be constituted by the light of the agent of the intellectual substance according to its act and essence. Let this wonderful philosopher imagine how such a form is constituted, unless it is constituted in particular. This is what is said in the Book of Causes[25], that intelligence knows lower things by virtue of being the cause of them.

If by chance he should say that the intellect, constituting its effects, does not know what it constitutes, this is completely ridiculous, because such a constitution is the operation of substance, which according to itself is the intellect, and is the operation of life and knowledge, and thus works and knows itself and its work and the work done. Therefore such a substance knows all that it does. And this is certainly the opinion of the Peripatetic philosophers. There are some who sophistically argue about the knowledge of God as about the knowledge of man do not understand the sayings of the philosophers.

Problem XI
What he does not know other than himself.

From the same things that have just been said, it is proved that what was stated in the eleventh is false. For from this the knowledge of God is constitutive of all things in being and form through light, which is itself what the Stoics called the idea. Yet, nothing is the principle of knowledge except that which is the principle of constitution, as the first statement of the book of the Physicists proves, and the light of the first understanding. It follows that God knows all things by that light which he is, and if he did not know in this way, it would follow that God had another, more divine intellect in understanding himself, through which his understanding would be perfected to act. Now that this is impossible is proved in *First Philosophy, XI*. Thus it follows from what has been said that God understands and knows everything by himself. Yet, since in

---

[25] A work that was, in the middle ages, attributed to Aristotle, but is likely a 9th century Arabic work by an unknown author.

everything that is known through something else from itself, it is not known except through that which is the principle of its own knowledge, and the thing known is different from the principle of knowledge itself. Therefore, it necessarily follows that in every type of knowledge of things known through something else from itself, something else is known. Another source of knowledge, that being God, therefore, by himself, as the principle of knowledge, knows something other than himself.

Now distinguish that certain things are known by themselves, and others by means of others, because of the simple things which are the principles of knowledge. For in these the known and the principle of knowledge are the same, and the same known in such things as are known by themselves. In this I thought that I was ignorant of no wise man among the philosophers. Therefore, God does not know by something other than Himself, yet He knows in many things something other than Himself.

Question XII

That human actions are not governed by the providence of God.

What is stated in the twelfth, namely, that the acts of man are not governed by the providence of God, is an ancient error of Tullius, who, although he had a wonderful mouth to speak wittily, yet had a heart of fools in philosophy, as something has been said of him before.

What is said is easily disproved. For there is nothing, according to Aristotle, in the order of causes, which is not referred to that which is before it in the same order, according to the government. When influence ceases in the former, causality ceases in the latter, as is proved in *Physics, VIII*, where the order of the movers and the moved is given. Man, then, who according to the order of his own providence is the master and cause of his actions, either has something before him or nothing, according to the order of providence. If it is said that he has nothing before him according to the order of providence, it follows that he is first in that order. The first is essentially operative in every order of causes. Man, therefore, by essence is provident and is providence itself, which is absurd. if he has before him another thing in the order of providence, it necessarily follows that in every work of his providence this is referred to another according to providence. Since the first in every order governs all that follows, it follows that man is governed in all his actions by divine providence. This is what is said in the *Book of Causes*, that "the first governs all things except that which is mingled with them," and that "the first is rich in itself" and in all other things.

Question XIII
That God cannot give immortality or incorruption to a mortal or corruptible thing.

What is stated in the thirteenth, namely, that God cannot give immortality and incorruption to a mortal and corruptible thing, is not a philosophical saying according to the philosophy of the Peripatetics, but philosophy must take the account of this saying from the Stoics.

Let us say, then, that the order of all orders is a certain order of its own. Now there is a corruptible and an incorruptible, as things that happen frequently, there is an order to things that are always, as is clear from what is well determined in the sixth book of the first philosophy.

Let us therefore inquire from these, what is the first cause of this order. Now it is agreed that in the first order there is a relation to the second. In the first, then, through the acting intellect, the reason for the order of all is, but every order is wise, as Aristotle says. From the order of the wise, then, some are far removed from the first, and some are not. From a distance it is caused that some are corruptible, and some are incorruptible. It is therefore from the order and power of the first ordainer that some are corruptible and some are not, and it is not from the matter and substance of the order except as from the consequent. First, the agent does not vary according to his power. Yet, God can still grant, as he could at first, that some things become corruptible from a great distance, and some things become incorruptible by the fact that in some way they are made nearest to the first. This is what Plato said: the gods of gods, whose father and maker I am, incorruptible by my will, but corruptible by nature. Hence it is also that certain wise men of the alchemists say that an elemental substance can be converted into quintescene by the fact that corruptible matter can be reduced to the disposition and order of incorruptibles.

Question XIV

The body of Christ lying in the tomb and placed on the cross is not, or was not, the same simply in number, but in what it is.

What is stated in the fourteenth, namely, that the body of Christ lying in the tomb and hanging on the cross is not the same simply in number, but in what it is, seems to be said because in others the inanimate body is equivalent to the animate body. To speak of the body of Christ through philosophy is rash, because it is not subject to human reason. However, even this statement is against the reason of the owner of the body. For in him was the power to lay down the soul and to take it up again by the power of the divinity hidden in himself. Therefore the soul of Christ, although it ceased from the body through death, yet never ceased from the divinity which was hidden in the body. Therefore he did not entirely cease from what was actually in the body. The body, therefore, even in the sepulcher, held the soul by the power of divinity. Therefore it was not one thing and another, but in the same number according to the being of the body, not simply, but in a certain way it was one thing and another. The sign of this is that the body of Christ could not experience corruption. This could not have been the cause, except that through death he did not cease from divinity, containing both body and soul. Of this, however, it is not expedient for a philosopher to speak much.

Question XV

That the angel and the soul are simple, but not with absolute simplicity, nor by approach to composition, but only by withdrawal from the highest simple.

Now in the fifteenth it is stated that the angel and the soul are simple, not simply or by absolute simplicity, nor yet that they are simple by approach to composition, but by withdrawal from the highest and first simple. It contains a contradiction of itself. For there can be no withdrawal from the highest and first simple except by an approach to composition. For either it departs by something different from the first simple, or it does not. For if it recedes through something, it follows that it is composed of like and unlike, according to its own substance and nature. If he proceeds through nothing, it necessarily follows that his simplicity is the first simplicity. If it is said, it follows that the second is the first, which is most inconvenient.

Furthermore, the orders of intelligences can only be distinguished by act and power, and such a power which determines the act of the first to be the second and third, and so on, as is clear to all who have read the sayings of the philosophers about the orders of intelligences. Much less, then, are the soul and the angel in their order determined to exist except by act and power, which determines that act to be according to substance. Therefore the angel and the soul are composite and not simple. But what such a composition is, has not been investigated, and therefore nothing needs to be said about this at present.

Of the fifteen problems enumerated above, these words are sufficient for the present intention.

Behold, this apologetic has been briefly conceived by us for the sake of corroboration, and has been extracted from the depths of philosophy, so that he who is ignorant of philosophy may not be found fit to read this.

LATIN TEXT

Venerabili in Christo patri ac domino Alberto, episcopo quondam Ratisponensi, frater Aegidius ordinis praedicatorum, licet indignus, cum salute "glorificare dominum in doctrinis". Articulos, quos proponunt in scholis magistri Parisienses, qui in philosophia maiores reputantur, vestrae paternitati tamquam vere intellectuum illuminatrici transmittens dignum duxi, ut eos iam in multis congregationibus impugnatos vos oris vestri spiritu interimatis.

Problema I

Quod intellectus omnium hominum est unus et idem numero.

Contra primum: Intellectum hominis secundum naturam et substantiam et diffinitionem cognoscere possibile non est, nisi et natura intelligentiae et natura et substantia animae et diffinitio cognoscatur. Loquimur enim hic de cognitione, quae est per philosophiam, et non de ea quae est secundum fidem et secundum theologiam. Quae quamvis omnibus certior sit, tamen, quia a multis non capitur, ideo putatur difficultates velle evadere, qui ad theologiam se confert. Ideo ex intimis philosophiae rationes assumentes de natura intellectus loquentes de intellectu loquemur.

In philosophia igitur PERIPATETICORUM non nisi duas novas positiones invenimus a se valde differentes et unam antiquam, in qua non differunt PERIPATETICI, sed omnes uniformiter conveniunt. Illa vero in qua omnes conveniunt, positio est ANAXAGORAE, qui loquens de intellectu possibili dicit, quod intellectus possibilis est separatus et immixtus, simplicissimus, nulli nihil habens commune. Propter quod QUIDAM opinati sunt ipsum esse unum et eundem in omnibus et nullo determinatum ad unum proprie, quo ad alterum non determinetur. Si enim ad unum aliquod determinetur, ut dicunt, illo necessario differt ab alio. Hoc autem quo determinatur, constat, quod non est de natura intellectus, quae omnibus est communis. Aut ergo non determinatur aut alio quodam determinatur. Si autem non determinetur, habetur propositum, scilicet quod unus et idem est in omnibus. Si autem alio quodam determinatur quod non est de natura intellectus, hoc videbitur esse contra hypothesim, quia cum nihil determinetur per aliquid quod sibi non est secundum aliquem modum immixtum, sequitur, quod intellectus alicui immixtus sit, quod non congruit positioni.

Adhuc autem, si intellectus aliqua natura determinetur ad aliquid, per illud disiungetur ab aliis omnibus illam naturam non participantibus. Cum omnis cognitio sit secundum similitudinem, sequitur, quod illorum a quibus disiungitur per dissimilitudinem, nullam penitus potest habere cognitionem. Hoc autem omnino falsum est, cum intellectus possibilis sit, quo est omnia fieri intelligibilia.

Adhuc autem, si aliquid materiae haberet intellectus possibilis, cum omnis potentia passiva, quae est materiae, per formam, quam recipit, formetur et distinguatur ad esse speciei per se vel per accidens, oporteret, quod intellectus ab omnibus a se receptis ad aliquod esse formaretur, quod in Theophrasto reprehendit ARISTOTELES . Et ideo dixerunt ANTIQUI, quod nihil omnium est intellectus quae recipit, eo quod universalia sunt per hoc quod sunt in ipso, quia universale, secundum quod universale, nulli penitus dat esse, sed potentiam quandam, sicut et ipsum universale potentia quadam existit et non actu ens secundum naturam. Exemplum huius dicebant visibile, secundum quod est in perspicuo. Hoc enim quia in perspicuo non est ut in potentia physice recipiente ipsum, ideo non accipit esse ab ipso sive per se sive per accidens. Perspicuum nec album est nec rutilum, sed potius est in ipso secundum esse, quod visibili confert perspicuum, et non secundum esse, quod accipit ab eo. Est enim visibile nihil aliud nisi color acceptus in esse simplici, quod habet a perspicuo secundum actum, quo perspicuum in actu est per lumen receptum in omnes partes ipsius in extremo et in profundo ipsius. Sicut et intellectus speculativus sive universale nihil aliud est nisi forma in simplicitate sua accepta secundum esse, quod a simplici habet intelligentia, cuius ipse est lumen et constitutio et hypostasis, sicut lumen corporale hypostasis colorum est et essentialis constitutio, quamvis lumen corporale vita non sit et ideo colores secundum operationem vitae non habeat. Lumen autem intelligentiae secundum actum vitae est et ideo secundum actum vitae formas habet intellectuales, quia intelligere est vivere, sicut dicit ARISTOTELES, et percipere intelligibilia in theoricis est vivere secundum intellectum. Et sicut visibile est in perspicuo, secundum quod perspicuum in actu luminis est determinatum ad terminum eius quod visu percipitur, ita etiam intelligibile in intelligentiae actu acceptum et ad terminos quiditatis et substantiae rei intellectae terminatum est universale, quod intelligitur.

Hoc igitur omnium Peripateticorum antiqua est positio, secundum quod eam ALFARABIUS determinavit. Ex qua sequitur intellectum possibilem intelligibilium omnium esse speciem et non omnino potentiam esse materialem ad ipsa. Et quia ad philosophos loquimur, qui talibus perfecte debent esse instructi, his amplius non insistimus.

Post hos Graeci sapientes, PORPHYRIUS scilicet et EUSTRATIUS, ASPASIUS et MICHAEL EPHESIUS et quam plures alii venerunt praeter ALEXANDRUM, qui EPICURO consentit, qui omnes intellectum hominis intellectum possessum et non de natura intelligentiae existentem esse dixerunt. Et quem Graeci sapientes possessum, eundem ARABUM philosophi AVICENNA, AVERROES, ABUBACHER et quidam ALII adeptum esse dicebant, quia id quod possessum est, aliud est et alterius naturae a possidente. Dicunt enim, quod cum anima intellectualis hominis sit imago totius orbis et sola omnis orbis capax et forma organico corpori deputata per naturae convenientiam, necessarium est ipsam esse imaginem intelligentiae illius quae est decimi orbis. Qui orbis est sphaera activorum et passivorum, cuius intelligentiae instrumenta sunt calidum et frigidum, humidum et siccum, rarum et densum et alia quae in elementis inveniuntur, non quidem secundum se, sed secundum quod haec a virtutibus caelestibus mota informantur. Imago autem talis intelligentiae non omnino potest esse pura et simplex, sicut est natura intelligentiae primae et simplicis. Si enim talis esset, non esset forma organica primo et per se, quia natura intelligentiae simplicis non est organica. Anima autem de natura sua est organica, et ab ea habet corpus, quod ipsum est organicum. Et ideo dicit AVERROES, quod omnis diversitas, quae est in corpore, est a diversitate, quae est in forma, sicut diversitas organorum est a diversitate potentiarum et virium, quae sunt in anima. Si enim anima sine potentiis secundum seipsam diceretur et quod a diversitate organorum corporis esset diversitas potentiarum, sequeretur, quod ipsa secundum se posset quolibet uti organo, cum secundum seipsam non esset magis determinata ad unum quam ad aliud. Et sic sequeretur tectonica tibicines indui et cetera inconvenientia, quae contra Pythagoram concludit ARISTOTELES.

Hac tali positione facta sequitur, quod sicut se habet intelligentia decimi orbis ad intelligentias orbium superiorum, ita se habet anima intellectualis, quae est in homine, ad intellectus orbium superiorum. Et ideo, sicut <in> intelligentia decimi orbis possessae et adeptae sunt formaliter intelligentiae superiorum, eo quod informant ipsam ad operationem intellectualem, ita in anima sunt lumina intelligentiarum adepta et possessa ab illustratione intelligibilium, et sicut intelligentia ultimi ordinis se habet ad potentias elementorum, sic se habet anima ad distinctiones et operationes organorum.

Si quis autem diceret, quod non est intelligentia, quae operatur in sphaera activorum, sed natura: quicumque hoc dicit, philosophiam nescit. Totum enim opus naturae probatum est esse opus intelligentiae per hoc quod cum ratione finis format et operatur diversa tam in plantis quam in animalibus et in omnibus quae perfectae sunt naturae; quod natura facere non potest, eo quod natura non est nisi ad unum. Propter quod etiam anima, quae non attingit perfectionem imaginis intelligentiae nisi ex parte illa qua intelligentia comparatur ad elementorum virtutes, sicut sensibilis et vegetabilis, a diversitate deprimitur ad unum et non sequitur diversitatem, quam imaginatur. Et ideo omnis hirundo ad unum modum facit nidum et omnis aranea similiter alii facit telam. Sed non omnis homo similiter alii facit domum vel vestem vel quodlibet aliud operum suorum.

Ex his et de necessitate sequitur intellectum hominis a tali natura animae quae organica est, esse possessum et adeptum a natura superiori; et quanto magis avertitur ab inferiori virtute, qua se habet ad organa, tanto magis intellectum suum proprium adipiscitur, acquirit et possidet; et quanto magis convertitur ad organa, tanto magis obumbratur et cadit ab intellectu et bestialis et arboreus efficitur et perdit intellectum et declinat a natura hominis. Et hoc est quod dicit ARISTOTELES, quod «secundum prudentiam dictus intellectus non aequaliter videtur inesse animalibus, sed neque hominibus». In hac autem adeptione nobilissima omnes Peripatetici radicem dixerunt esse immortalitatis et per ipsam homines in deos transponi et transformari, et tales PLATONIS philosophia heroas quasi semideos appellavit.

Ex his autem facile convincitur, quod cum illud quod est imago intelligentiae ex ea parte qua comparatur ad qualitates elementares, nec unius naturae sit nec unius potentiae nec unius puritatis, quod anima unius non est anima alterius, igitur possidens in uno non idem quod possidens in alio. Si autem hoc concedere necessarium est, cum secundum possidentia et adipiscentia secundum esse differant possessa et adepta, sequitur necessario, quod intellectus possessi et adepti secundum esse singulariter differant in quolibet. Cuius exemplum valde conveniens est, quod dicit ARISTOTELES in II DE ANIMA: Quamvis enim perspicuum sit in igne et aere et aqua et quibusdam lapidibus et vitro ex convenientia cum perpetuo superius corpore, tamen secundum esse singulare differt in quolibet ipsorum.

Secundum hanc igitur positionem non sequitur, quod unus numero intellectus secundum esse sit in omni homine, sed quod potius secundum esse singulariter differat in quolibet ipsorum. Utrum autem in omnibus orbibus sint intelligentiae differentes secundum substantiam aut in omnibus sit lumen primae causae operans ad modum intelligentiae, differens in illis secundum esse, quod habet in illis, sicut videtur sentire AVENALPETRANS, ad praesens non est tempus discutere, quia quodlibet istorum dicatur, semper habetur de necessitate, quod non unus intellectus possibilis numero est in omnibus hominibus, et hoc hic intendimus.

AVICEBRON autem in libro, quem FONTEM VITAE appellavit, alia via processit. Quamvis enim PERIPATETICUM se profiteretur, tamen STOICORUM et praecipue PLATONIS dogma secutus est, ex uno tamquam paterno intellectu volens producere omnia. Propter quod triplicem distinxit materiam, scilicet eam quae prima determinatur forma substantiali, et eam quae determinatur prima forma corporali, et eam quae determinatur prima contrarietate. Primam autem formam dicit esse intellectivam sive intellectualitatem, ex qua dicit multiplicatas esse substantias intellectuales et animas; quantitate autem dicit determinatam materiam corporum caelestium; et contrarietate dicit determinatam esse materiam physicorum generabilium et corruptibilium. Et secundum huiusmodi positionem planum est omnem intellectualem naturam in hoc vel in illo acceptam esse singularem nec unum intellectum numero esse in aliquibus pluribus.

Ex omnibus positionibus constat hoc falsum esse etiam secundum philosophiam, quod unus numero intellectus secundum esse acceptus sit in omnibus, et plus sequitur etiam hoc quod dicunt, non esse intelligibile, quia communis animi conceptio est, quam GRAECI axioma vocant, quod quidquid secundum esse est in multis, multiplicatur in illis, et esse, quod habet in uno, non habet in alio.

Quod autem ANAXAGORAS dicit, quod nulli nihil habet commune, de natura et essentia intellectus dictum est et non de esse. Constat enim, quod secundum esse intellectus coniungitur continuo et tempori, et quod coniungitur continuo et tempori, multis et multis modis est immixtum. Et omnium horum exemplum est natura perspicui in caelo et igne et aere et aqua, lapidibus et vitro.

Non ergo tantum secundum theologos falsum est, quod dicunt, sed etiam secundum philosophiam; sed causa dicti est ignorantia philosophorum, quia multi PARISIENSES non philosophiam, sed sophismata sunt secuti.

Haec ergo responsio ad primum.

Problema II

Quod ista est falsa vel impropria: homo intelligit.

Secundum est, quod dicunt hanc falsam vel impropriam: «homo intelligit». Quod non dixit, nisi qui philosophiae et sui ipsius habuit ignorantiam, quia in philosophia determinatum est, quod homo solus est intellectus et quod intelligere propria et connaturalis est operatio hominis, quae si non sit impedita, summa est hominis felicitas. Per quod patet nullam in mundo adeo propriam sicut hanc: «homo intelligit». Cum enim proprium sit, quod omni convenit et soli et, sicut dicit BOETHIUS, quod proprium de substantia manat et substantialibus, non est proprium hominis sentire et vegetari, sed solum intelligere.

Adhuc autem, cum non sit propositio verior quam illa in qua connaturalis et proprius actus attribuitur illi cuius est proprius et connaturalis, manifestum est nullam inter omnes propositiones esse veriorem quam istam: «homo intelligit», sicut cum dicitur: lux lucet, et albedo visum disgregat, calidum calet et cetera huiusmodi; nisi forte velit dicere intellectum nihil esse hominis, quod valde est absurdum. Sequitur enim id quo homo homo est, nihil esse hominis, quod numquam aliquis opinatus est, quia hoc intelligibile non est. Omne enim quod ab aliis sui generis speciebus distinguitur, oportet, quod aliqua differentia ultima et convertibili, quam essentialiter participat, distinguatur ab aliis, ut inevitabiliter in VII PRIMAE PHILOSOPHIAE probatum est. Intellectuale autem est ultima hominis differentia, ut omnes Stoici et Peripatetici confitentur.

Si forte dicant, quod intellectuale inest homini ut natura et potentia, sed actum et operationem non habet in ipso, hoc omnino absurdum est, quia sequitur, quod natura propria destituatur operatione, quod absurdum est.

Si autem forte dicant, quod ratiocinari actus proprius hominis est et non intelligere, hoc valde imperiti hominis non dictum, sed figmentum est. Quia si quis subtilius ista intuetur, ratiocinatio numquam fit, nisi intellectu componente et dividente informetur; est igitur intellectus secundum naturam et rationem; magis ergo proprium est homini intelligere quam ratiocinari.

Si autem velit dicere, quod intelligere superiori naturae convenit ut angelicae et ideo inferiori non potest esse proprium, primum quidem contra hoc est, quod philosophus extra metas philosophiae fugit, quia non est philosophicum. Distinctiones enim angelorum per revelationem spiritus et non per philosophiam sunt acceptae. Si autem dicat, quod secundum philosophiam sunt intelligentiarum ordines, et illis et non homini convenit intelligere, et hoc iterum absurdum est, quia nihil prohibet id quod per analogiam dicitur, proprium esse pluribus diversis modis. Si vero hoc intendatur, quod quidam ARABUM PHILOSOPHI dixerunt, intellectum alicuius agentem esse extra animam, qui est ut sol et ut «ars ad materiam sustinuit», hoc valde debile dictum est, quia hoc dato non sequitur, quod homo <non> intelligat proprie et vere. Quia quamvis illa intelligentia quae est ut sol solus lucens et ad esse et lucere omnia formans et sicut ars materiae formas artis ex seipsa influens, tamen influentia luminis illius intelligentiae per esse est in anima et ita informat animam ad intellectum et operationem intellectus, sicut sol omnia informat lucentia ad illuminationis formam et operationem. Et sicut illa proprie et vere dicuntur luminaria et lucendi actum habentia, ita proprie dicuntur intellectuales et operationem intellectus habentes, quia id quod est actus superioris, non prohibet secundum esse participatum esse differentiam substantialem naturae inferioris, sicut patet in omnibus quae per formam et substantiam generant. Adhuc tamen quamvis sustinendo positionem ita dicamus, tamen non est probatum hoc quod dicunt, verum esse.

Absurdum est ergo omnimodo hoc quod dixerunt in secunda fictione.

Problema III

Quod voluntas hominis ex necessitate vult et eligit.

Quod autem tertio dicunt, quod voluntas hominis ex necessitate vult et eligit, numquam potuit dicere nisi homo penitus illitteratus, quia omnis ratio et omnis ethicorum schola tam Stoicorum quam Peripateticorum clamat nos dominos esse actuum nostrorum et ideo laudabiles vel vituperabiles. PHILOSOPHI autem de natura animae sermocinantes in hoc a natura distinguunt animam, quia natura est ad unum per se, anima vero plurium per se operativa et etiam contrariorum et contradictoriorum electiva. Quorum nihil verum est, si homo ex necessitate vult, quod vult, et eligit ex necessitate, quod eligit.

Adhuc, si verum est, quod dicunt, iam voluntas non est voluntas, quod patet in HERMETE TRISMEGISTO et ARISTOTELE et in omnibus qui in decem ordinibus causas distinxerunt, in qua distinctione semper voluntas a necessitate distincta est.

Adhuc, secundum hoc fortuna non est de his quae fiunt a proposito, quia fortuna non admittit necessitates, et sic magna pars SECUNDI PHYSICORUM falsa est.

Et quod coniungunt electionem voluntati, quae numquam est voluntatis, non fuit philosophicum et, ut breviter dicatur, ita absurdum est illud, quod non est dignum responsione.

Si autem hoc dicunt propter fatum et constellationem, quam poeta dicit necessario trahere voluntatem - dicit enim POETA: «Te tua fata trahunt, ne coepta relinquere possis» - hoc dictum imperitorum est et malitiae solacium. Probatum est in principio libri, qui arabice ALARBA, latine autem QUADRIPARTITUM vocatur, quod fatum, quod ex constellatione est, necessitatem non imponit propter tres causas. Quarum una est, quia non immediate, sed per medium advenit, cuius inaequalitate impediri poterit; secunda autem, quia per accidens, sed non per se operatur in natis; operatur enim per primas qualitates, quae non per se virtutes stellarum accipiunt; tertium est, quod operatur in hoc in quod operatur, in diversitate et potestate materiae natorum, quae materia uniformiter et, prout sunt in caelis, recipere non potest caelorum virtutes. Omni ergo modo ridiculosum est, quod dicunt.

Problema IV

Quod omnia quae in inferioribus aguntur, subsunt necessitati corporum caelestium.

Id vero quod quarto inducunt, quod omnia quae in inferioribus aguntur, necessitati subsunt corporum caelestium, eundem fere habet modum improbationis. Hoc tamen mirabile est, quod philosophiae professores contra ea dicunt quae in philosophia probata sunt. Si enim VI LIBER PRIMAE PHILOSOPHIAE legitur, facile patet, qualiter ea quae in inferioribus aguntur, superiorum subsunt regimini. Ibi enim ostenditur, qualiter id quod in naturalibus causis frequenter est et non semper et ubique, cadit ab eo quod semper est, et non assequitur necessitatem eius quod semper est. Probatur etiam, qualiter id quod raro est in casu et fortuna, cadit ab eo quod frequenter est, et non assequitur ordinem eius. Et ut omnino pateat eorum ignorantia, in II DE GENERATIONE ET CORRUPTIONE probatum est, quod quamvis allatio solis et planetarum in circulo declivi sit causa generationis inferiorum et recessus eorundem in eodem circulo sit causa corruptionis et sint aequales periodi generationis et corruptionis: tamen inferiora periodi aequalitatem et ordinem non assequuntur propter materiae inaequalitatem et inordinationem. Quis autem dubitet propositum hominis magis inaequale et inordinatum esse quam naturae? Multo minus ergo propositum necessitati subiacet quam natura.

Sed quia, ut dicit ARISTOTELES, non sufficit falsum ostendere, nisi etiam causa falsitatis ostendatur, ideo resumentes dicimus, quod anima humana secundum PHILOSOPHOS est imago mundi. Propter quod in ea parte qua imago intelligentiae et causae primae est, impossibile est eam motibus caelestium subiacere. In ea autem parte qua in organis est, quamvis sidereis moveatur scintillationibus, tamen necessitatem et ordinem superiorum non assequitur, et sic nec in illa parte necessitati subiacet vel subditur superiorum. Probatur autem hoc a HALY in COMMENTO SUPER CENTILOQUIUM PTOLEMAEI, qui dicit de rege, cuius omnes significatores mali et immundi erant, et tamen natus in tali constellatione mundissime vixit, fulgens vestitu et gloria, cum optimis conversationem ducens. Cuius causa cum a Haly quaereretur, respondit, quod quidem ad immunda ex desiderio traheretur, sed videns, quod talis esset inhonesta conversatio, ut dominus actuum suorum talia fugiens elegit honestatis conversationem.

Aliud exemplum in PHYSIONOMIA POLI de HIPPOCRATE. HIPPOCRAS enim in omnibus signis corporis, quae stellas secundas vocat PTOLEMAEUS, scortator et turpis apparebat, et tamen optimorum erat studiorum et honestissimae conversationis in tantum, ut omnium hominum optimus diceretur, quod fieri non potuit nisi per honestatis electionem. Necessitatem ergo in inferioribus superiora non imponunt, nec umquam hoc aliquis dixit mathematicorum. Si enim hoc esset, periret casus, periret liberum arbitrium, periret consilium et periret contingens secundum omnem ambitum suae communitatis, quod est valde absurdum.

Problema V

Quod mundus est aeternus.

Quod autem mundus sit aeternus, sicut quinto inducunt, antiqua valde quaestio est, quamvis ex probatione ARISTOTELES haberi non possit, sed quod a nullo generante motus primus factus sit et a nullo physice corrumpente possit desinere. Hoc autem optime improbat MOYSES AEGYPTIUS in libro, qui DUX NEUTRORUM vocatur. Quamvis enim ea sint ingenerabilia et incorruptibilia, quae ex tota sua sunt materia, tamen innegabile est, quod omnis multitudo in omnibus motibus ordinata ad unum ab uno primo, qui causa ordinis illius est, sit causata. Omnis autem multitudo orbium et stellarum in omni motu suo ad unum et idem respicit, respectu cuius secundum formas omnia mobilia mutantur continue, quamvis secundum se tota et secundum omnes partes non moveantur secundum locum. Hoc autem est centrum et polus uterque. Centrum enim et poli ad unum et eundem axem, quem meguar ASTRONOMI vocant, referuntur. Huius ergo ordinis de necessitate causa est aliqua, quaecumque sit illa.

Probatum autem est, quod motus localis non est nisi a generante aliquo, quod dando formam dat motum. Igitur id quod motum caelestibus attribuit, oportet, quod sit generans ea secundum materiam et formam. Caelum igitur cum omnibus quae in ipso sunt, genitum est secundum substantiam et naturam, et sic positio, quam dicunt, improbata est.

Si autem dicat aliquis, quod hoc est verum in his quae moventur naturaliter et non de his quae moventur ab anima, hoc nihil est, quia motus superiorum non solum est ab anima secundum eos qui superiora animas habere contendunt. Si enim ab anima sola esset et non a natura, etiam corporum lassitudinem induceret secundum eos etiam qui huius positionis sunt professores. Cum ergo naturae corporalis sit idem motus sicut consequens naturam et formam eorum, sequitur de necessitate, quod ante iam conclusum est.

Propter quod etiam ipsi philosophi, ut AVICENNA et ALGAZEL, dicunt non esse prohibitum, quin mundus per creationem factus sit, quamvis motus et mobile primum non sint facta per generationem physicam et quamvis non sint desinentia per physicam corruptionem. De hac autem quaestione in ALIIS SCRIPTIS a me plura sunt, et ideo ista sufficiant.

Ad hoc tamen etiam valet, quod in II ARITHMETICAE probatum est in loco, qui invictus vocatur, quod scilicet omnis multiplicitas ad unitatem reducitur, quae causa substantialis est multiplicitatis illius. Quaeramus ergo, ad quid ante se omnis reducitur caelorum et stellarum et motuum multiplicitas. Et cuilibet patet, quod reduci non potest nisi ad primi motoris unitatem, quam omnes inferiores in motibus suis secundum aliquid desiderant.

Si autem subtiliter inspiciatur, quae causa sit illius difformis desiderii, non potest aliquis dicere, quod alia sit nisi similitudo imperfecta ad causam primam. Non enim aliquid appetit aliud nisi per similitudinem, quam habet ad aliud; nec aliquid movetur ad aliquid nisi propter imperfectionem, quam habet in illo quod appetit. Similitudo igitur primi, quae est in omnibus et multiplex est, in illis causari non potuit nisi per hoc quod omnia sunt ab illo. Omnium enim quorum est similitudo essentialis ad unum, fluxus est ab uno aliquo, in quo illud in quo similia sunt, actu est et perfectum. Sic species a genere, sic sunt individua a speciebus, sic omnis multiplicitas trahit se in unitatem. Quaeramus ergo ab istis, si hoc aliquis capere posset intellectus, quod primum omnibus hanc influat similitudinem iam existentibus in natura et esse; et constat, quod hoc non est intelligibile. Oportet ergo, quod hanc similitudinem causavit in omnibus, causans omnia secundum essentiam et in esse naturali et substantiali. Omnia ergo ab uno perfecta sunt secundum substantiale esse et naturale. Facta sunt ergo omnia secundum esse. Non ergo hoc modo sunt aeterna, quod principium essendi secundum substantiam et naturam non habuerunt.

Problema VI

Quod numquam fuit primus homo.

Sextum, quod proponunt, non est philosophicum. Philosophi enim est id quod dicit, dicere cum ratione. Neutrum autem probari potest, scilicet quod numquam fuerit primus homo et quod aliquando fuerit primus homo. Et cum neutrum probari possit ratione perspecta, tamen probabilius est aliquando fuisse unum primum hominem quam non fuisse, quia quorum est una natura communis, horum est unus ingressus in esse illius naturae, nisi sint nata per putrefactionem. Homo autem sicut nec aliquod perfectorum animalium non est de his quae nasci possunt per putrefactionem, sicut dicit AVERROES super XI METAPHYSICAE. Igitur nullus hominum naturaliter in esse hominis ingressus est nisi per generationem. In omni autem generatione determinatum est generans. Quilibet igitur homo determinatum habet generantem. Omne autem determinatum generans aliquando fuit in tempore signato. Omnis ergo homo aliquando fuit in tempore signato. Ex infinito autem nihil est accipere signatum. Quia autem quaelibet sunt infinita, quae non contingit pertransire usque ad hoc signatum, igitur in his quae signata et determinata sunt, non est ponere infinitum, sed necesse est ponere aliquod primum.

Si forte dicat, quod ex constellatione diversae generationes fiant in diversis habitationis principiis, hoc iterum est contra philosophiam, quae dicit perfectissima animalia ex solis constellationibus nasci non posse. Propter quod PLATO in PRIMO TIMAEI LIBRO et OVIDIUS loquentes de diluviis elementorum, quae fiunt propter stellarum exorbitationem, reservatos dicunt Pyrrham et Deucalionem, ex quibus futurum semen reservaretur humanae generationis. Et cum homo sit imago causae primae, probabilius est constitutum primum hominem esse a causa prima, quam aliter in esse processisse.

Et ut utamur probabilitate ipsius ARISTOTELES, quam TULLIUS ponit in I LIBRO DE NATURA DEORUM, ubi verba ARISTOTELIS inducit dicens, quod si in deserto ex improviso stans inveniatur palatium, in quo non nisi hirundines inveniantur, quamvis nesciatur artifex, qui fecit palatium, tamen ex ipse palatii dispositione statim convincitur, quod hirundines illud palatium non fecerunt, sed aliqua natura intellectualis per rationem artis fecit illud. Ita etiam cum mundus artis opus sit et rationis et in ipsis generatis non possit consistere, <non> nisi probabile est, quod primae generatorum substantiae per rationes dei deorum in esse sunt productae. Et haec pro certo ARISTOTELIS est philosophia, quam vulgarem ipse vocat in I libro DE CAELO ET MUNDO. Rationabilius ergo est, quod primus homo per creationem constiterit, quam quod numquam fuerit primus homo.

Problema VII

Quod anima, quae est forma hominis, secundum quod homo, corrumpitur corrupto corpore.

Quod autem septimo dicunt animam, quae est forma hominis secundum quod homo corrumpi corrupto corpore, ex omnimoda philosophiae procedit ignorantia, quia secundum PHILOSOPHOS nulla, quae vere forma est, corrumpitur, quia in materia nulla est. Ea enim quae in materia est, aut imago formae est aut resonantia.

Adhuc, si ea solum vere forma est, quae non est actus alicuius materiae, sequitur solum intellectum vere formam esse, eo quod nullius corporis actus est. Intellectus autem forma hominis est, ut homo est, qui separatur ut incorruptibile a corruptibili. Forma ergo hominis, ut homo est, corruptibilis non est.

Si autem volunt dicere animam esse, quae est corporis entelechia vel actus, omnino ignorantiae dictum est, quod dicunt. Anima enim entelechia corporis est per actum suum substantialem, quae est vita, sicut patet ex alia diffinitione animae, quae est «demonstratio positione differens», quae est: quod «anima est principium et causa vitae, secundum quod vivere viventibus est esse». Et tamen non omnes partes corporis uno modo participant vitam, sed quaedam ad nutriri et vegetari, quaedam autem ad sentire et quaedam plus, quaedam minus, tamen omnia participant vitam.

Quaeramus ergo, utrum participant vitam intellectus vel non. Et si dicatur, quod non, sequitur necessario animam, quae est forma hominis, corpus habere ad sensum et vegetationem et non ad intellectum. Corpus igitur hominis non erit animae rationali proprium, et sic sequitur «tectonica tibicines indui».

Propter quod necesse est dicere, quod omnia membra vivunt anima rationali, sicut omnia instrumenta textoris formantur ad textoris operationem, et quod sensus in homine non forma est, sed potentia animae rationalis, et idem oportet dicere de vegetativa. Et hinc est, quod caro hominis differt specie a carne aliorum animalium.

Ex hoc autem sequitur, quod aut tota corrumpitur secundum actum substantialem aut, si salvatur secundum substantiam, quod etiam salvetur secundum totum illud quod est forma hominis, ut homo est. Salvatur autem secundum substantiam, ut dicit ARISTOTELES in XI METAPHYSICAE et in multis aliis locis, et nos probavimus hoc in LIBRO DE IMMORTALITATE ANIMAE. Oportet ergo, quod secundum omnia salvetur, quae in ipsa sunt ut potentiae ipsius. Est autem vegetativum in sensibili et sensibile in rationali «sicut trigonum in tetragono». Salvatur ergo vegetabile et sensibile per aliquem modum. Non autem aliter salvari possunt, nisi prout sunt in rationali ut potentiae ipsius. Salvatur ergo anima hominis, prout in ipsa est vegetativum et sensitivum, non ut actus, sed ut potentia rationalis animae.

Hoc ergo dictum non erat dictum sapienter, quia tota anima hominis etiam in ossibus non est forma hominis, nisi prout est rationalis, vitam rationis omnibus influens membris. Propter quod dicit ARISTOTELES manum esse organum intellectus. Et sicut non nisi forma intellectus est in securi et ascia et dolabra et in auro, lignis et lapidibus, ita forma animae rationalis prout forma rationalis est in omnibus membris humani corporis. Quae quidem separatur secundum substantiam et quandam operationem, in operationibus autem quibusdam separatur secundum potentiam et non secundum operationem, sicut et ars separatur a securis operatione et asciae, quamvis salvetur secundum potentiam. Hoc ergo dictum non fuit secundum philosophiam.

Utrum autem anima corruptibilis sit vel non, ad propositam non pertinet intentionem, quia non de natura quaerimus, sed contra positionem quandam disputamus. Haec autem causa est, quod THEOLOGI dicunt etiam corpora humana ab immortali anima potentiam accipere ad incorruptionem. Nulla enim forma est, quae non totam materiam sibi debitam ad esse proprium formae et actum et operationem non perficiat et terminet. Nec huius propositionis invenitur instantia. Omne igitur quod actu est pars hominis, ad esse animae rationalis et actum et operationem animae rationalis est determinatum; unde vegetata caro vegetatione hominis ad actum vivi rationalis est vegetata et sensus sentit ad actum vivi rationalis; aliter enim intelligere intelligentibus non esset esse, quod est inconveniens, quia in NATURALIBUS probatum est, quod, sicut vivere viventibus est esse et sentire sentientibus, ita intelligere est esse intelligentibus. Separatur autem anima rationalis sicut incorruptibile a corruptibili. Aut ergo separatur secundum totam substantiam suam aut secundum partem suae substantiae. Nec potest dici, quod secundum partem suae substantiae separatur, quia nihil simplicium, hoc est non quantorum, secundum partem suae substantiae separatur, nec intelligi potest, quod pars substantiae separetur et non totum in talibus, quae non mole quantitatis distenduntur. Separatur ergo tota substantia animae, quae est forma humani corporis, quamvis in separata anima aliquae potentiarum non separentur secundum esse, quod habent in corpore, sicut patet per antedicta.

Si autem isti antiqui erroris novi vellent esse discipuli, qui a PLATONE derivatus est, et dicere velint, quod vegetabilis et sensibilis et rationalis tres sint substantiae, quae sunt in homine, facile hoc eliditur per PRIMAM PHILOSOPHIAM. Secundum hoc enim diffinitio hominis, qua dicitur vivum, sensibile et rationale, esset multa et non unum. Sic enim dicendo, vivum non est in sensibili per esse sensibilis et sensibile non est in rationali per esse rationalis, sed tres erunt substantiae distinctae, quarum nulla per esse est in alia. Quod si dicatur ab aliquo, ille propter ignorantiam a scholis philosophiae est eiciendus, quia talis pro certo ignorat ipsa philosophiae principia.

Si autem dicatur, quod ipse PHILOSOPHUS dicat in XI METAPHYSICAE, quod non tota anima hominis separatur, pro certo hoc non dicit PHILOSOPHUS propterea, quod non tota substantia separatur, sed quia non tota separatur secundum esse potentiarum.

Problema VIII

Quod anima post mortem separata non patitur ab igne corporeo.

Dicunt octavo, quod anima separata post mortem non patitur ab igne corporeo. Sed hoc nullo modo est philosophicum, cum tamen a SOCRATE in FINE LIBRI, qui PHAEDON appellatur, infernalia distincta sunt loca poenarum et fluvii infernales et loca bonorum interlucentibus gemmis adornata. Quem modum etiam imitatus est ISAAC in LIBRO DE DIFFINITIONIBUS et multi poetarum etiam talia loca cantaverunt cantu philosophico, qui fabula vocatur.

Dicant ergo isti, si anima rationalis aliquid patitur in corpore vel non. Et si quidem non patitur, tunc penitus est impassibilis homo doloris, cum tamen dolor sit sensus contrarii dissolventis. Si autem patitur, constat, quod corporeo affligente patitur. Cum ergo sit extra corpus eiusdem naturae cuius est in corpore, constat, quod etiam extra corpus ab affligente corporeo pati potest.

Si forte dicunt, quod anima in corpore habet contrarium, sed non exuta corpore, istud secundum omnem philosophiam verum non est, quia in PHI LOSOPHIA determinatum est, quod finis prosperitatis animae separatae, quae est ultima felicitas, est in hoc quod coniungitur primo motori. Constat autem, quod secundum omnes STOICOS peccatum est, quod a primo motore disiungit, et hoc coniunctioni est contrarium. Habet igitur anima exuta aliquid contrarium. Sicut ergo dolet de contrario in corpore, ita dolet de contrario extra corpus.

Adhuc autem probari non potest, quod anima non doleat de affligente corporaliter, quia hoc est contra sensuum experimentum. Apprehensio autem affligentis ut affligentis facit internum animae dolorem. Ergo etiam apprehensio affligentis extra corpus facit internum animi dolorem. Quae ergo est causa, quod dicatur, quod exuta non doleat de affligente corporeo? Et hoc est quod dicit GREGORIUS, quod hoc est in igne ardere quod ignem videre, hoc est ut affligens apprehendere.

Si autem dicere velit, quod corporale ad dolorem animalem agere non potest, hoc penitus absurdum est, quia in calore naturali, qui ignis est, videmus actiones ad sensum animae et delectando et tristando, quia quamvis sit igneus talis calor, tamen ab anima informatus et motus ad animae agit operationes et passiones. Quid ergo prohibet ignem corporeum a primo motore vim accipere, inquantum est instrumentum eius, quod agat in animam animali et non corporali actione vel passione? Nec aliquid talium est contra philosophiam Stoicorum vel etiam Peripateticorum, sed talia aut ex ignorantia aut certe ex odio fidei procedunt magis quam ex probata veritate.

Problema IX

Quod liberum arbitrium est potentia passiva, non activa et quod de necessitate movetur ab appetibili.

Quod vero nono dicunt liberum arbitrium esse potentiam passivam et non activam et ideo de necessitate moveri ab ipso appetibili, omnino absurdum est et contra principia ethicorum philosophorum. Acceptivae enim dicuntur illae potentiae quae passivae vocantur in anima, sicut patet in libro DE ANIMA III. Acceptio numquam sine actione perficitur, et ideo tales potentiae simpliciter passivae esse <non> possunt. Tales enim potentiae suo et de suo conferunt formis, quae in ipsis sunt, sicut perspicuum suo et de suo confert formae visibilis, quod est in ipso secundum esse luminis et perspicui tantum.

Et hoc modo intellectus et omnis acceptionis pars confert formae et agit in ea veritatem et simplicitatem, qua in ipso est forma intelligibilis. Et cum intellectus de appetibili in appetitum faciat nuntium, constat, quod etiam de eo quod est appetitus, confertur appetibili, quod ipsum est in appetitu. Talis autem operatio a PHILOSOPHIS actus perfectus et non imperfectus esse dicitur, quia motus non esset alicuius actus imperfectus, nisi esset etiam alicuius actus perfectus. Est enim actus perfectus motoris et agentis, imperfectus autem mobilis et patientis. Cum igitur principia constituentia formam prout intellectualis et appetibilis sint ipsius intellectus et appetitus, tales potentiae, a quibus fluunt talia formarum principia, potius sunt activa quam passiva, et quod plus est, simpliciter sunt activa et secundum quid sunt passiva. Haec autem causa est, quare nos sumus domini actuum nostrorum. Principium ergo talium in nobis et a nobis est. Non ergo necessario movetur ab appetibili.

Adhuc autem talis pseudophilosophus destruit continentiam et totum librum VII ETHICAE NICOMACHICAE, quia continens passione turpi movetur, sed non deducitur, abstinens ab insecutione passionum per liberum arbitrium. Contingit autem illi error sicut et THEOPHRASTO, quia scilicet passiones animae ad passiones physicas mensurantur, cum nihil simile habeant cum ipsis, sicut omnibus planum est, qui ethicas bene sciunt philosophias.

Problema X

Quod deus non cognoscit singularia.

Quod autem decimo dicitur, quod deus singularia non cognoscit, ex omnimoda procedit ignorantia. Supponitur enim, quod scientia dei ad scientiam hominis sit univoca, quod in PRIMA PHILOSOPHIA est improbatum. Scientia enim mea omnis causatur ex rebus scitis ideo, quia ex rationibus rerum et passionibus causatur omnis nostra scientia. Propter quod omnis scientia melior est resolutionis scientia, quam analyticam GRAECI vocant, dum vel compositum in simplex vel causatum in causam vel generaliter posterius resolvitur in prius. Compositionis enim scientia in homine causatur a resolutiva, quia componere nescit, nisi qui novit componentia et proportiones componentium ad invicem et ad composita. Unde necesse est resolutionis scientiam primam esse, secundo autem eam quae est compositionis. Omnis autem resolutio perficitur abstractione. Hominis igitur scientia est per abstractionem. Abstractio autem a rebus fit nec aliter fieri potest. Scientia ergo hominis causatur a rebus. Scientia autem dei non a rebus fit, sed est rerum causa. Constat enim omnem formam esse lumen intelligentiae, quia cum omnis forma detur ab intellectu, qui secundum substantiam et essentiam intellectus est, et non ab intellectu, qui adeptus vel acquisitus vel possessus vocatur a PHILOSOPHIS, oportet, quod omnis forma causetur ab intellectu universaliter agente omnes omnium intelligibilium formas. Hoc autem qualiter fiat, non est possibile nisi hoc modo, quod ipsum lumen intellectus agentis forma sit eius quod per intellectum interius, qui universaliter agens est, constituitur. Intellectus autem omnis qui rem in esse constituit et forma, primo est ad particulare, secundo ad universale, in quo natura agit occulta per consequens. Intellectus ergo dei et scientia divina primo sunt de particulari, et si sunt de universali, hoc erit non primo, sed per consequens. Hoc enim vult dicere PHILOSOPHUS, quando dicit, quod talis intellectus est ut sol et «ut ars ad materiam sustinuit». Sol enim constitutivus est visibilium in particulari et ars constitutiva artificialium in particulari et non in universali nisi per consequens.

Amplius, omnis forma rei per hoc intellectui adepto sive possesso intelligibilis efficitur, quod ipsa est lumen agentis intellectus, qui proprius actus est intellectus possibilis, sicut omnis color est visibilis, quia est actus lucis solis, qui proprius actus est potentiae visivae. Oportet igitur omnem formam a lumine agentis intellectualis substantiae constitutam esse secundum actum et essentiam. Fingat igitur iste mirabilis philosophus, qualiter forma talis constituitur, nisi in particulari constituatur. Et hoc est, quod in LIBRO DE CAUSIS dicitur, quod intelligentia scit res inferiores per hoc quod est causa earum.

Si forte dicat, quod intellectus constituens sua effecta non cognoscit ea quae constituit, hoc omnino ridiculum est, quia talis constitutio operatio est substantiae, quae secundum seipsam est intellectus et est operatio vitae et cognitionis taliterque operans et se cognoscit et opus suum et operatum. Scit ergo talis substantia omnia quae operatur. Et hoc pro certo philosophorum sententia est Peripateticorum. Sed quidam sophistice de scientia dei sicut de scientia hominis disputantes non intelligunt dicta philosophorum.

Problema XI

Quod non cognoscit alia a se.

Ex eisdem autem quae nunc dicta sunt, falsum esse probatur id quod undecimo positum est. Ex quo enim scientia dei rerum omnium in esse et forma constitutiva est per lumen, quod ipsa est, quod ideam Stoici vocabant, nihil autem principium cognitionis est, nisi idem quod est principium constitutionis esse, sicut probat prima propositio libri PHYSICORUM, lumen autem primi intellectus simplicis et agentis principium constituens est in esse formali: sequitur, quod deus illo lumine quod ipse est, omnia cognoscat et nisi ita cognosceret, sequeretur, quod deus alium diviniorem se intellectum in intelligendo haberet, per quem suus intellectus in intelligendo perficeretur ad actum. Quod autem hoc impossibile sit, probatum est in PRIMAE PHILOSOPHIAE libro XI. Sic ex dictis sequitur deum omnia intelligere et scire seipso. Cum autem in omni eo quod cognoscitur per aliud a seipso, non cognoscatur nisi per hoc quod est principium suae cognitionis, res autem cognita aliud sit ab ipso cognitionis principio: sequitur necessario, quod in omni cognitione rerum per aliud a se cognitarum aliud sit cognitum, aliud cognitionis principium. Deus ergo per se, ut cognitionis principium, aliud a se cognoscit.

Distingue autem, quod quaedam per se, quaedam per aliud a se cognoscuntur propter simplicia, quae sunt cognitionis principia. In his enim idem est cognitum et cognitionis principium, et idem cognitum in talibus quae a seipsis cognoscuntur. In hoc autem nullum sapientem in philosophicis ignorare putabam. Deus ergo si non cognoscit per aliud a seipso, cognoscit tamen in plurimis aliud a seipso.

Problema XII

Quod humani actus non reguntur providentia dei.

Quod autem duodecimo ponitur, scilicet quod humani actus providentia dei non reguntur, error antiquus est TULLII, qui quamvis os haberet ad lepide loquendum mirabile, tamen cor habuit fatuum in philosophia, sicut QUIDAM ante nos dixerunt de ipso.

Facile autem improbatur, quod dicitur. Nihil enim est secundum ARISTOTELEM in ordine causarum, quod ad id quod est ante se in eodem ordine, secundum regimen non referatur; et cessante influentia in priori, cessat causalitas in posteriori, sicut probatur in VIII PHYSICORUM, ubi ordo ponitur moventium et motorum. Homo ergo, qui secundum ordinem suae propriae providentiae est dominus et causa suorum actuum, aut secundum ordinem providentiae habet aliquid ante se aut nihil. Si dicatur, quod nihil habet ante se secundum providentiae ordinem, sequitur, quod est primum in ordine illo. Primum autem in omni ordine causarum est essentialiter operans. Homo igitur per essentiam est providens et est ipsa providentia, quod est absurdum. Si autem aliud in ordine providentiae habet ante se, sequitur necessario, quod hoc in omni opere providentiae suae ad aliud secundum providentiam referatur. Cum autem primum in omni ordine regat omnia sequentia, sequitur, quod homo in omnibus actibus suis a providentia divina regatur. Et hoc est, quod dicitur in LIBRO DE CAUSIS, quod «primum regit res omnes praeter hoc quod commisceatur cum eis» et quod «primum est dives in se» et in omnibus aliis.

Problema XIII

Quod deus non potest dare immortalitatem vel incorruptibilitatem rei mortali vel corruptibili.

Quod autem decimo tertio ponitur, scilicet quod deus dare non possit rei mortali et corruptibili immortalitatem et incorruptibilitatem, non est dictum philosophicum secundum philosophiam Peripateticorum, sed oportet huius dicti rationem ex Stoicorum accipere philosophia.

Dicamus ergo, quod ordinum omnium ordinatorum ratio est aliqua sui ordinis; est autem corruptibilium et incorruptibilium, sicut eorum quae frequenter fiunt, est ordo ad ea quae sunt semper, sicut patet in his quae in VI libro PRIMAE PHILOSOPHIAE bene sunt determinata.

Quaeramus ergo ab his, quae sit prima causa ordinis istius. Constat autem, quod in priori ratio ordinis est ad secundum. In primo ergo per intellectum agentem ratio ordinis est omnium; sed omnis ordo sapientis est, ut dicit ARISTOTELES. Ex ordine ergo sapientis est quaedam longe a primo distare et quaedam non. Sed ex longe distare vel non distare causatur quaedam esse corruptibilia, quaedam esse incorruptibilia. Ex ordine ergo et potestate primi ordinantis est, quod quaedam sunt corruptibilia, quaedam autem non, et non est a materia et substantia ordinatorum nisi sicut ex consequenti. Primum autem agens non variatur secundum posse. Potest autem adhuc deus dare, sicut primo potuit, quod quaedam fiant corruptibilia per longe distare et quaedam incorruptibilia per hoc quod per aliquem modum propinquissima efficiuntur ad primum. Et hoc est, quod dixit PLATO: dii deorum, quorum pater opifexque ego, voluntate mea incorruptibiles, corruptibiles autem natura. Hinc est etiam, quod QUIDAM ALCHIMICORUM sapientes elementalem substantiam in caelum dicunt posse converti per hoc quod materia corruptibilis potest reduci ad incorruptibilium dispositionem et ordinem.

Problema XIV

Quod corpus Christi iacens in sepulchro et positum in cruce non est vel non fuit idem numero simpliciter, sed secundum quid.

Quod autem decimo quarto ponitur, quod scilicet corpus Christi iacens in sepulcro et suspensum in cruce non sit idem numero simpliciter, sed secundum quid, ideo dictum videtur, quod in aliis corpus exanime aequivocum est ad corpus animatum. Sed de corpore Christi loqui per philosophiam temerarium est, eo quod rationi humanae non subicitur. Tamen etiam hoc dictum contra rationem est corporis domini. In ipso enim fuit potestas ponendi animam et iterum sumendi eam virtute latentis in se divinitatis. Anima ergo Christi, quamvis per mortem destiterit a corpore, tamen numquam destitit a divinitate, quae latebat in corpore. Non ergo in toto destitit ab eo quod fuit actu in corpore. Corpus igitur etiam in sepulchro potestate divinitatis tenuit animam. Non ergo fuit aliud et aliud, sed idem numero secundum esse corporis non simpliciter, sed modo quodam fuit aliud et aliud. Huius autem signum est, quod corpus Christi corruptionem experiri non potuit. Et huius causa esse non potuit, nisi quia per mortem non destitit a divinitate, et corpus et animam continente. De hoc tamen non multum loqui expedit philosopho.

Problema XV

Quod angelus et anima sunt simplices, sed non absoluta simplicitate nec per accessum ad compositionem, sed tantum per recessum a summo simplici.

Quod autem decimo quinto ponitur angelum et animam esse simplices non simpliciter sive absoluta simplicitate, neque tamen simplices esse per accessum ad compositionem, sed per recessum a summo et primo simplici: in seipso sui ipsius habet contradictionem. Nullo enim modo potest esse recessus a summo et primo simplici nisi per accessum ad compositionem. Aut enim per aliquid dissimile recedit a primo simplici aut non. Si enim per aliquid recedit, sequitur, quod constans ex simili et dissimili compositum est secundum sui ipsius substantiam et naturam. Si autem per nihil recedit, sequitur necessario, quod simplicitas eius sit prima simplicitas. Quod si dicatur, sequitur, quod secundum est primum, quod inconvenientissimum est.

Adhuc autem, ordines intelligentiarum distingui non possunt nisi actu et potentia, et tali potentia, quae actum primi determinat ad esse secundi et tertii et sic deinceps, sicut patet omnibus, qui dicta philosophorum legerunt de ordinibus intelligentiarum. Multo minus ergo anima et angelus in ordine suo determinantur ad esse nisi per actum et potentiam, quae actum illum ad esse determinat secundum substantiam. Ergo angelus et anima composita sunt et non simplicia. Quae autem sit talis compositio, non est inquisitum, et ideo de hoc nihil est dicendum ad praesens.

De quindecim ergo problematibus in ante habitis numeratis ista dicta sufficiant ad praesentem intentionem.

Ecce istud apologeticum a nobis breviter propter corroborationem conceptum est et de intimis philosophiae extractum, quo is qui philosophiam ignorat, ad legendum hoc idoneus non inveniatur.

Other Translations by D.P. Curtin:

First Book of Ethiopian Maccabees: with additional commentary (Dec. 2018)
The Protoevangelium of James: Greek and English Texts (July 2019)
The Old Nubian Miracles of St. Mena (Jan. 2021)
Exhortation to Monks ordained in India by *St. John of Karpathos* (Mar. 2021)
On God by *Eznik of Kolb* (Sept. 2021)
Esoteric Canons and Triodia by *St. Andrew of Crete* (Nov. 2021)
On the Work of Monks by *St. Oriesius of Tabenna* (Dec. 2021)
About Fifteen Problems by *St. Albertus Magnus* (Feb. 2022)
Testament of Some Former Things by *John Scotus Eriugena* (Mar. 2022)
The Georgian Synaxarium (Aug. 2022)
Instructions: Counsel for Novices by *St. Ammonas the Hermit* (Sept. 2022)
Book on Religious Exercise and Quiet by *St. Isaiah the Solitary* (Oct. 2022)
The Syriac Menologium and Martyrology (Nov. 2022)
Vision of Theophilus by *St. Cyril of Alexandria* (Dec. 2022)
On Fate (De Fato) by *St. Albertus Magnus* (Feb. 2023)
Fragments of 'Chronicle' by *Hippolytus of Thebes* (May 2023)
The Syriac Life of John the Baptist by *Serapion the Presbyter* (June 2023)
The Life of the Blessed Theotokos by *Epiphanius Monachus* (July 2023)
Second Book of Ethiopian Maccabees: with additional commentary (Aug. 2023)

www.ingramcontent.com/pod-product-compliance
Lightning Source LLC
Chambersburg PA
CBHW070942120626
46546CB00004B/1518